"This series is a tremendous resource fo   ble with an
understanding of how the gospel is wc   ɔel-minded
pastors and scholars doing gospel businᴄ   al and theological feast preparing God's people to apply the entire Bible to all of life with heart and mind
wholly committed to Christ's priorities."
   BRYAN CHAPELL, Chancellor, Covenant Theological Seminary

"Mark Twain may have smiled when he wrote to a friend, 'I didn't have time to write you a
short letter, so I wrote you a long letter.' But the truth of Twain's remark remains serious and
universal, because well-reasoned, compact writing requires extra time and extra hard work.
And this is what we have in the Crossway Bible study series *Knowing the Bible*. The skilled
authors and notable editors provide the contours of each book of the Bible as well as the
grand theological themes that bind them together as one Book. Here, in a 12-week format,
are carefully wrought studies that will ignite the mind and the heart."
   R. KENT HUGHES, Senior Pastor Emeritus, College Church, Wheaton, Illinois

"*Knowing the Bible* brings together a gifted team of Bible teachers to produce a high-quality
series of study guides. The coordinated focus of these materials is unique: biblical content,
provocative questions, systematic theology, practical application, and the gospel story of
God's grace presented all the way through Scripture."
   PHILIP G. RYKEN, President, Wheaton College

"These *Knowing the Bible* volumes provide a significant and very welcome variation on the
general run of inductive Bible studies. This series provides substantial instruction, as well as
teaching through the very questions that are asked. *Knowing the Bible* then goes even further
by showing how any given text links with the gospel, the whole Bible, and the formation of
theology. I heartily endorse this orientation of individual books to the whole Bible and the
gospel, and I applaud the demonstration that sound theology was not something invented
later by Christians, but is right there in the pages of Scripture."
   GRAEME L. GOLDSWORTHY, former lecturer, Moore Theological College; author,
   According to Plan, Gospel and Kingdom, The Gospel in Revelation, and *Gospel and Wisdom*

"What a gift to earnest, Bible-loving, Bible-searching believers! The organization and
structure of the Bible study format presented through the *Knowing the Bible* series is so well
conceived. Students of the Word are led to understand the content of passages through per-
ceptive, guided questions, and they are given rich insights and application all along the way
in the brief but illuminating sections that conclude each study. What potential growth in
depth and breadth of understanding these studies offer! One can only pray that vast numbers
of believers will discover more of God and the beauty of his Word through these rich studies."
   BRUCE A. WARE, Professor of Christian Theology, The Southern Baptist Theological
   Seminary

KNOWING THE BIBLE

J. I. Packer, Theological Editor
Dane C. Ortlund, Series Editor
Lane T. Dennis, Executive Editor

•   •   •   •   •   •

Genesis	Matthew	Galatians
Exodus	Mark	Philippians
Ruth/Esther	Luke	Colossians/Philemon
Psalms	John	Hebrews
Proverbs	Acts	James
Isaiah	Romans	Revelation
Daniel	1 Corinthians	

•   •   •   •   •   •

J. I. PACKER is Board of Governors' Professor of Theology at Regent College (Vancouver, BC). Dr. Packer earned his DPhil at the University of Oxford. He is known and loved worldwide as the author of the bestselling book *Knowing God*, as well as many other titles on theology and the Christian life. He serves as the General Editor of the ESV Bible and as the Theological Editor for the *ESV Study Bible*.

LANE T. DENNIS is President of Crossway, a not-for-profit publishing ministry. Dr. Dennis earned his PhD from Northwestern University. He is Chair of the ESV Bible Translation Oversight Committee and Executive Editor of the *ESV Study Bible*.

DANE C. ORTLUND is Senior Vice President, Bible Publishing, at Crossway. He is a graduate of Covenant Theological Seminary (MDiv, ThM) and Wheaton College (BA, PhD). Dr. Ortlund has authored several books and scholarly articles in the areas of Bible, theology, and Christian living.

1 CORINTHIANS

A 12-WEEK STUDY

Jay Thomas

CROSSWAY

WHEATON, ILLINOIS

Crossway is a publishing ministry of Good News Publishers.

VP		25	24	23	22	21	20	19	18	17	16	15
15	14	13	12	11	10	9	8	7	6	5	4	3	2	1

TABLE OF CONTENTS

SERIES PREFACE

KNOWING THE BIBLE, as the series title indicates, was created to help readers know and understand the meaning, the message, and the God of the Bible. Each volume in the series consists of 12 units that progressively take the reader through a clear, concise study of that book of the Bible. In this way, any given volume can fruitfully be used in a 12-week format either in group study, such as in a church-based context, or in individual study. Of course, these 12 studies could be completed in fewer or more than 12 weeks, as convenient, depending on the context in which they are used.

Each study unit gives an overview of the text at hand before digging into it with a series of questions for reflection or discussion. The unit then concludes by highlighting the gospel of grace in each passage ("Gospel Glimpses"), identifying whole-Bible themes that occur in the passage ("Whole-Bible Connections"), and pinpointing Christian doctrines that are affirmed in the passage ("Theological Soundings").

The final component to each unit is a section for reflecting on personal and practical implications from the passage at hand. The layout provides space for recording responses to the questions proposed, and we think readers need to do this to get the full benefit of the exercise. The series also includes definitions of key words. These definitions are indicated by a note number in the text and are found at the end of each chapter.

Lastly, for help in understanding the Bible in this deeper way, we would urge the reader to use the ESV Bible and the *ESV Study Bible*, which are available online at www.esvbible.org. The *Knowing the Bible* series is also available online. Additional 12-week studies covering each book of the Bible will be added as they become available.

May the Lord greatly bless your study as you seek to know him through knowing his Word.

J. I. Packer
Lane T. Dennis

WEEK 1: OVERVIEW

▲

Getting Acquainted

The apostle[1] Paul's epistle[2] to the Corinthian church covers many different theological and practical questions, but there is one central issue he is addressing, and that is unity. The Corinthian church was fractured, and the chief reason was pride. This pride manifested itself in a skewed view of the gospel,[3] which led to sinful attitudes about things such as speech and knowledge, and a misuse of their spiritual gifts.

Like many churches today, the Corinthian church was very gifted. They were intellectually sharp; some were financially blessed; they were variously talented and had very visible and powerful gifts from the Holy Spirit. Yet those gifts were not submitted to the greatest of the Spirit's purposes in human lives, namely, love. Paul argues throughout this letter that Christ-exalting, cross-defined love must replace the puffed-up pride that coursed through this church. In fact, a key principle in 1 Corinthians is that giftedness without character leads to bondage and sin, not freedom and redemption.

At the heart of this book is the reality of the cross and resurrection. Paul admonishes this church to return to the logic and pattern of the gospel, so that pride is replaced with servant-hearted love and unity.

Placing It in the Larger Story

First Corinthians is one of Paul's letters to a first-century church in ancient Corinth. Jesus had completed his earthly ministry, had died on a cross for the sins of the world, had been raised from the dead in fulfillment and victory, and had returned to his Father in heaven. The Spirit had been given in full at Pentecost, and the church had begun to grow throughout Asia Minor, with both Jews and Gentiles being brought in. This letter is one of many epistles written to local churches that were growing and wrestling with what it means to be faithful communities of Christ's followers. Each church had unique questions and struggles, and the church at Corinth was no exception. This letter addresses a fundamental and ongoing issue for any local church: how does the gospel unite God's people in humility and love?

 Key Verse

"So now faith, hope, and love abide, these three; but the greatest of these is love." (1 Cor. 13:13)

Date and Historical Background

The apostle Paul wrote this letter to the Corinthian church sometime between 53–55 AD, toward the end of his three-year ministry in Ephesus. First Corinthians is actually one of several letters exchanged with this church, but only 1 and 2 Corinthians survive as part of the inspired canon of the Bible.

The ancient city of Corinth, home of the church to which Paul addressed this letter, was formerly a Greek settlement and had been rebuilt after a devastating war in 146 BC. It was a port town and was situated along a trade route. Corinth was prosperous, what we might refer to today as an economically resourceful, bourgeois, new-money town. With those characteristics came cultural dilemmas for the church, which was made up mostly of Gentile converts. Among these challenges were the lure of wealth, social elitism, and rampant sexual temptations tied to paganism. This was a church of new believers who struggled to transcend the values of the Hellenistic, pagan world.

Paul sternly, but pastorally, exhorted this church to seek the better way, the way of Christ-centered, humble, loving unity built upon the cross-cultural reality of the gospel.

Outline

   I. Epistolary Introduction to the Letter's Main Themes (1:1–9)

     A. Greeting: apostleship, sanctity, and unity (1:1–3)

     B. Thanksgiving: speech, knowledge, and spiritual gifts (1:4–9)

As You Get Started

What is your understanding of how 1 Corinthians helps us to grasp the identity and role of Christ's church? What in your view does 1 Corinthians uniquely contribute, theologically and practically, to our understanding of a truly Spirit-filled, faithful local church, as well as the Spirit-filled life of the individual believer?

What is your current understanding of what 1 Corinthians contributes to Christian theology? How does this letter clarify our understanding of Christian unity, the role of preaching, church leadership, sexual ethics, principles for worship gatherings, the place and role of spiritual gifts, Christian freedom and conscience, the bodily resurrection of Jesus, and other truths?

What aspects of 1 Corinthians have confused you? Are there any specific questions about church life and personal discipleship that you hope to have answered through this study?

▶ **As You Finish This Unit . . .**

Take a moment now to ask for the Lord's blessing and help as you engage in this study of 1 Corinthians. And take a moment also to look back through this unit of study, to reflect on a few key things that the Lord may be teaching you—and perhaps to highlight or underline these to review again in the future.

Definitions

[1] **Apostle** – Means "one who is sent" and refers to one who is an official representative of another. In the NT, refers specifically to those whom Jesus chose in his lifetime to represent him; and Paul, whom Jesus encountered and commissioned on the Damascus road.

[2] **Epistle** – Essentially synonymous with "letter." A literary form common in NT times. Epistles typically included: (1) designation of the author and recipient; (2) brief greetings and expressions of thanks; (3) the body of the letter; (4) personal greetings and signature; and (5) a closing doxology or blessing. Twenty-one books of the NT are epistles.

[3] **Gospel** – The common translation for a Greek word meaning "good news," referring specifically to the good news of Jesus Christ and the salvation he made possible by his crucifixion, burial, and resurrection. *Gospel* with an initial capital letter refers to any of the four biblical accounts of Jesus' life on earth (Matthew, Mark, Luke, and John).

WEEK 2: INTRODUCTION: SPEECH, KNOWLEDGE, AND SPIRITUAL GIFTS

1 Corinthians 1:1–9

The Place of the Passage

Paul begins this letter in classic form, with initial greetings and a highlighting of the issues that will arise as key themes throughout the letter, including the theme of unity. Paul identifies himself and his intended audience, and portrays the Corinthian church as those sanctified[1] in Jesus and in fellowship with all the saints who call upon the name of the Lord (1:2). Paul then shifts to words of thanksgiving as he addresses three key themes in the letter: speech, knowledge, and spiritual gifts (1:5–7). This initial greeting is sincere but also pointed. Paul uses it as a means to point to the grace and salvation the Corinthian believers possess, yet also as a means to exhort them toward obedience in areas where they are clearly walking in sin.

The Big Picture

First Corinthians 1:1–9 reveals that God's people are first and foremost defined by the peace and grace given to them through Jesus, which in turn is a basis and mandate for their sanctification.

> ### Reflection and Discussion

Read through the complete passage for this study, 1 Corinthians 1:1–9. Then review the shorter sections below and write your own notes concerning this introductory section. (For further background, see the *ESV Study Bible*, page 2192, or visit www.esvbible.org.)

1. Greeting (1:1–3)

Paul begins by identifying himself and Sosthenes. What does it mean that Paul was "called" as an apostle? Why is it important that he mentions this?

We don't know much about Sosthenes (Acts 18:12–17 may be describing the same man), but why might it be significant that Paul mentions this ministry partner? How does partnership in ministry help frame the main idea of unity in this letter?

Several key terms, such as *sanctified*, *called*, *saints*, *grace*, and *peace*, are introduced by Paul. How do these terms set the stage for what is to come (feel free to read the next section, to get the context)? In a first-century secular letter, an introductory blessing would often be, "Peace and health." Notice that Paul says, "Grace and peace." How is that significant?

2. Thanksgiving (1:4–9)

Speech, knowledge, and spiritual gifts arise as three key themes here, in preparation for and anticipation of the rest of the letter. Notice how Paul comments on each in verses 5–7. Is Paul condemning the existence of these three realities in the lives of the Corinthians? If not, how is he shaping their view of each reality?

What is the greater reality to which Paul is calling these Christians at the end of verse 7? How does that set the perspective the Corinthians should have toward their blessings and talents?

In a culture of elitism, where social standing was everything, how does the theme of being called to Christ provide a challenge and new framework for these believers to think about their community and their individual lives?

Read through the following three sections on *Gospel Glimpses*, *Whole-Bible Connections*, and *Theological Soundings*. Then take time to reflect on the *Personal Implications* these sections may have for your walk with the Lord.

Gospel Glimpses

MINISTRY AS PARTNERSHIP. Paul begins by mentioning Sosthenes, a man who was significant enough to be described as a brother and a fellow source of this letter. We do not know for sure, but this might be the same man mentioned in Acts 18:12–17, a ruler of the synagogue in Corinth who was beaten for not repudiating Paul. In the very first verse we see how a gospel perspective on life leads to a partnership model, rather than a solo model. Solo leaders tend to be about self. Partnerships exemplify the unity and beauty of a community who serve Jesus for his glory.

GRACE AND PEACE. Secular letters often begin with a blessing formula of "peace and health." The New Testament letters change that to "grace and peace." In classic Pauline style, the opening verses are filled with gospel language that inspires the recipients to embrace a Christ-centered perspective before Paul dives into the main ideas. Because the Corinthian situation is one of pride that breaks down unity, the very nature of grace is radically important. When God's people realize that they are great sinners who have encountered an infinite Savior, pride naturally crumbles.

CALLED TO CHRIST. In a society where social standing matters supremely, one's abilities and résumés are often idols. One-upmanship, constant self-justification, and self-righteousness abound in cultures of elitism. That is why Paul focuses us on our calling. Those who are called, forgiven, and given all grace cannot claim any merit in themselves. That is humbling, and that is what proud folk such as the Corinthians, and we, desperately need. The gospel does not take high-caliber applicants with great references. The gospel calls sinners, who without it have no hope.

Whole-Bible Connections

A PEOPLE CALLED TO HOLINESS. Throughout the Old Testament, God called those whom he loved to be his children and to be a part of his mission. In Genesis 12, God called Abraham to himself and also to a mission to extend his promises to a nation and then to the world. It is no surprise, then, to see that New Testament believers are also called. Paul is called as an apostle (1 Cor. 1:1), but then he describes the Corinthians as having been called to be saints (v. 2). This calling is not just to fellowship with God through Jesus, although that is primary; it is also a call to new identity and mission. It is a continuation of Israel's story, for Israel was called and then commissioned in Exodus 19:5–6 to be a kingdom of priests and a holy nation. First Peter 2:9 cites this passage from Exodus and applies it to the church. We are called to God and called to his mission to make his glory known in all the world.

DAY OF THE LORD. The day of the Lord is a key theme in the Old Testament. Israel longed for the arrival of this day, on which God would come to save and judge. That day arrived, in one sense, when the Son of God became incarnate as a man and lived among us. The cross was and is the high point of salvation and judgment. But in another sense, the Bible teaches that the day of the Lord—what our passage refers to as the "revealing of our Lord Jesus Christ" along with "the day of our Lord Jesus Christ" (1 Cor. 1:7–8)—is still to come. Like the Old Testament saints, the church must live a life of faith and obedience as we wait for Jesus' return. This faith in a certain future is not only a comfort but also a summons to intensity, as the days are short and we must urgently live for Christ.

▶ Theological Soundings

SANCTIFICATION. Sanctification is the work of the Holy Spirit to conform believers more fully to the image of Christ. In this passage we see that the church is comprised, necessarily, of people who are being "sanctified in Christ Jesus" (1:2). Thus, the Spirit uses the person and work of Jesus as the basis to make us more holy. Likewise, along with drawing us closer to the purposes of God, sanctification in Christ by the Spirit draws us closer to other believers, as we see in the rest of verse 2. As Paul makes clear, sanctification draws our hearts to Jesus and drives us to call upon him constantly.

SOVEREIGNTY. The thrust of these first nine verses is the almighty initiative of God in calling us to faith, bestowing grace, revealing himself in Christ, and giving spiritual gifts. God's initiative is also clearly evident here in the way he sanctifies us, sustains our faith, and promises to return to us in welcoming love, having established us as guiltless. The doctrine of God's sovereignty can easily become abstract and seemingly irrelevant. But Paul sets the foundation of his letter by describing the Christian life as one defined not just by grace but by *sovereign* grace. This in turn is radically practical as it gives life to the Christian pattern of humility and unity among and with other believers.

Personal Implications

Take time to reflect on the implications of 1 Corinthians 1:1–9 for your own life today. What did you learn; how have you been shaped; how might you walk more fully trusting the Lord Jesus? Make notes below on the personal implications for your walk with the Lord of the (1) *Gospel Glimpses*, (2) *Whole-Bible Connections*, (3) *Theological Soundings*, and (4) this passage as a whole.

1. Gospel Glimpses

2. Whole-Bible Connections

3. Theological Soundings

4. 1 Corinthians 1:1–9

▶ As You Finish This Unit . . .

Take a moment now to ask for the Lord's blessing and help as you continue in this study of 1 Corinthians. And take a moment also to look back through this unit of study, to reflect on some key things that the Lord may be teaching you—and perhaps to highlight and underline these things to review again in the future.

Definitions

[1] **Sanctification** – The process of being conformed to the image of Jesus Christ through the work of the Holy Spirit. This process begins immediately after regeneration and continues throughout a Christian's life.

WEEK 3: THE ISSUE OF DISUNITY

1 Corinthians 1:10–17a

The Place of the Passage

First Corinthians 1:10–4:21 is the larger unit that explores the presenting issue of divisions over loyalty to different Christian preachers. Our first sub-unit is 1:10–17a, wherein Paul declares how unity is being compromised in the Corinthian church. He says that it has been reported to him that "there is quarreling among you, my brothers" (1:11b). Specifically, there are factions in the church, aligned along loyalty lines toward certain well-known preachers, such as Paul, Cephas (Peter), Apollos, and even Christ himself. A theme of identification emerges in this paragraph: the kind of leaders with whom we identify can have a significant impact on our sense of unity. A divided church reveals that it has removed its focus from the gospel and thus has become bereft of "the same mind and the same judgment" (1:10). Here, the theme of gospel proclamation, and what it actually is, is introduced (see chapters 2–3).

The Big Picture

First Corinthians 1:10–17a shows that the Corinthian church was clearly disunited and quarreling, as a spirit of competitiveness had crept in, ironically finding expression in loyalty toward various Christian preachers.

> ## Reflection and Discussion

Read through the complete passage for this study, 1 Corinthians 1:10–17a. Then review the questions below and write your notes on them concerning this first movement of the main body of the letter. (For further background, see the *ESV Study Bible*, pages 2192–2193, or visit www.esvbible.org.)

1. Divisions (1:10–12)

Paul appeals to the Corinthians in the name of the Lord Jesus Christ. Why is the name of Jesus not merely a formula of authority but also a theologically important reality to bring up at this point?

Paul urges the Corinthians to agree together, to be united in the same mind, and even to have the same judgment. Is Paul commanding this church to have absolute uniformity of opinion and belief? If not, what does he mean by such vivid terminology?

What is the connection between loyalty to Christian leaders, especially inspiring ones, and potential disunity? Look at the way Paul rhetorically phrases this problem in the Corinthian church in verse 12. How does that phraseology help identify how human loyalty and potential disunity can go hand in hand?

2. Identification (vv. 13–17a)

Paul asks the Corinthians, "Is Christ divided?" (1:13). What does he mean by that, given the context?

Paul then evokes the images of crucifixion and baptism. How do those in turn relate to the presenting issue of divisions over Christian preachers? What is it about those two issues that gets at the heart of unity?

Baptism is a beautiful and glorious gift from God that symbolizes the work of the gospel in regenerating[1] us. How is baptism coming into play here? Are there areas in the contemporary church that are similar, calling for a response similar to Paul's?

How would eloquent communication skills inadvertently play into the current divisions in the Corinthian church?

Read through the following three sections on *Gospel Glimpses, Whole-Bible Connections*, and *Theological Soundings*. Then take time to consider the *Personal Implications* these sections may have for you.

Gospel Glimpses

UNITY IN CHRIST. Paul is creative in how he employs images of the lordship of Christ, the cross, and baptism to make it utterly clear that true unity can be found only in Christ. The fact that many Corinthians are divided along loyalty lines to perceived celebrity preachers was a sign that their eyes were no longer on Jesus. Even those who professed allegiance to Christ were apparently doing so out of conceit, not humility. When Paul speaks of agreement and like-mindedness and of having the same judgment (1:10), it is radical Christ-centeredness that Paul has in view. He is not speaking of total uniformity in all things, but rather of a robust unity of belief and focus on Jesus and his gospel.

THE PRIORITY OF THE CROSS. Paul addresses the problem of human hero worship, and how it distorts unity, in the context of baptism. Some of the Corinthians were bragging about who had baptized them (in this case Paul) as if baptism, and who administered it, created a badge of distinction and so was a matter for pride. It could not be more the opposite. Baptism is a sign and seal of the work of Christ. Paul is beginning to correct the Corinthians by redefining the ministry of preaching and the significance of baptism by pointing back to their ultimate referent, the cross of Christ. Indeed, Paul is not satisfied with rebuking the disunity itself, but he points to the causal issue, namely, a lack of focus on the cross itself. Therefore, baptism is important but not to be confused with the power of the gospel itself, which flows from the cross of Christ. This prepares us for what follows in the text.

Whole-Bible Connections

GRUMBLING AND MURMURING. The storyline of the Bible has some quite obvious patterns. One is that when God's people stop trusting in God's word, they begin to quarrel. Perhaps the most obvious Old Testament example is that of Israel with Moses. This pattern continues into our day. The Corinthian church had taken its eyes off Jesus and the glory of the cross. Therefore, they were disunited and even at odds with each other, taking gifts that God had given them to promote the gospel, such as godly preachers and baptism, and ironically twisting these into obstacles to unity. Paul is quick to point this out and to exhort the church to focus on Jesus himself and his work. Unity will then come.

IDENTITY MARKERS. While water baptism was a sign and seal given to God's people in the new covenant,[2] this was not the first time God had chosen to mark his people with an outward symbol to identify them as his own possession. In Genesis 3, God marked Adam and Eve with the skins of animals, replacing their feeble fig leaves. In Genesis 17 God gave the mark of circumcision to Israel to identify them as his covenant people. In 1 Corinthians 10:2, Paul says that Israel was baptized into Moses, meaning that as they passed through the Red Sea they were identified with Moses, the servant of God, and thus were saved from the slavery of Egypt. All of these symbols and marks were important, but in each case the actual person of God and his work was the power behind the symbol. The symbol showed the world that a person belonged to God and his purposes, but all the attention and glory were to be given to God.

> ### Theological Soundings

BAPTISM. Baptism is a gift, and it was commanded by Jesus as the initiatory sign and seal of becoming a disciple (Matt. 28:19). While baptism is commanded, and therefore disregard of it is disobedience to Jesus' command, it is not necessary for salvation. Different Christian traditions vary on some of the nuances of the administration and implications of baptism, yet almost all agree that it is an outward sign of an inward reality, and it is a physical representation of the work of the gospel in the life of the converted believer. In Romans 6, Paul speaks of it as the symbol of death to the old life and resurrection to the new life in Christ. Therefore, water baptism is a very important step of obedience for every believer to take.

THE CROSS. The implications of the cross are too many to name. Our eternal worship will never plumb the depths of its truth and beauty. But in our passage, Paul uses the cross to rebuke and encourage the Corinthians back toward unity. He simply asks, was Paul crucified for you? In other words, did the Corinthians not understand that Christ's work on the cross is to be their focal point, and that it should draw all people together? This reality helps us know how to appreciate gifted preachers and Christian ordinances such as baptism. While both of those are wonderful and admirable, we must respect their purpose, and that is to draw us back to the glory of the cross itself. The cross is to be the power of preaching, the significance of baptism, and the basis of Christianity. When the cross is that central in local churches, competitiveness, grumbling, and unholy allegiances dissolve away.

▶ Personal Implications

Take time to reflect on the implications of 1 Corinthians 1:10–17a for your own life today. What did you learn; how have you been shaped; how might you walk more fully trusting the Lord Jesus? Make notes below on the personal implications for your walk with the Lord of the (1) *Gospel Glimpses*, (2) *Whole-Bible Connections*, (3) *Theological Soundings*, and (4) this passage as a whole.

1. Gospel Glimpses

2. Whole-Bible Connections

3. Theological Soundings

4. 1 Corinthians 1:10–17a

As You Finish This Unit . . .

Take a moment now to ask for the Lord's blessing and help as you continue in this study of 1 Corinthians. And take a moment also to look back through this unit of study, to reflect on some key things that the Lord may be teaching you—and perhaps to highlight and underline these things to review again in the future.

Definitions

[1] **Regeneration** – The Holy Spirit's work of bringing spiritual life to a person, thus enabling him or her to trust, love, and follow God. Essentially equivalent to what is often referred to as being "born again," or "saved."

[2] **New covenant** – The old and new covenants mark the two major divisions of the history of salvation. The old covenant was the era under the law of Moses, marked by God's particular work with the nation of Israel and the typological system of priesthood, sacrifice, and local presence that he gave them. The new covenant was prophesied about repeatedly and was ushered in by the ministry of Christ, with the moment of transition occurring at Pentecost as the Holy Spirit was given in his fullness to the church.

Week 4: Proclamation, Wisdom, and Unity

1 Corinthians 1:17b–4:21

The Place of the Passage

Paul embarks on perhaps the most theologically and pastorally important section of the letter. First Corinthians 1:17b–4:21 is the anchor of the epistle. The problem of disunity has been reported, and now the spiritual causes are named. This, in turn, sets the stage for the *answer* to the problem to be named as well. The problem is the wisdom of the world. The answer is the wisdom of God. Paul turns human and worldly sensibility on its head in several distinct areas in these verses. He essentially calls the Corinthians "backwards" in their manner of approaching reality. The Corinthians have been taking their cues from the culture around them, and it is now time for them to take their cues from the logic of the gospel, not least the reality of the cross. This section highlights the purpose of preaching, the role of the Christian leader, the issue of true power, and the place of suffering—not ease—in gospel ministry.

The Big Picture

In 1 Corinthians 1:17b–4:21 Paul exhorts the people of God to reclaim true Christian unity by embracing Christ crucified as the solution to their quarreling and competitiveness, because Christ crucified is the logic of all of spiritual life.

Read through the complete passage for this study, 1 Corinthians 1:17a–4:21. Then review the questions below and write your notes on them concerning this larger section, broken down into the nature of God's wisdom (1:17b–2:16) and God's wisdom applied to the human preachers and the Corinthians themselves (3:1–4:21). (For further background, see the *ESV Study Bible*, pages 2193–2196, or visit www. esvbible.org.)

1. The nature of God's wisdom (1:17b–2:16)

Human wisdom is about strength found in this world, about power advantage, about prestige, and about looking good in front of others. How does Paul unsettle these notions? Look at Isaiah 29:14, quoted in 1:19. How does the context of Isaiah and that quote support Paul's point?

A key historical background key to a better understanding of the Corinthian situation and Paul's response is the Greco-Roman valuation of rhetoric.[1] Ancient rhetoricians were professional traveling speakers who thrilled crowds with their use of words. Their purpose was to persuade a crowd toward a viewpoint. The viewpoint per se was not crucial, but rather the persuading itself was the point. These speakers used words in such a way as to delight and move their audience. The power was in the words and human giftedness. The rhetorician did not even necessarily need to believe the viewpoint he was advocating. How is Paul contradicting all of this? How was Paul's self-conception different (see 1:18–2:5)?

If Paul is not a typical rhetorician, and his aim is to convey a message about Jesus and the cross, then he must be more akin to a prophet or herald. Given what we learn in 1:17b–2:16, what is the job description of the faithful herald of the gospel?

How does Paul define true wisdom? How is the cross essential to the argument and profoundly evocative of true wisdom?

2. God's wisdom applied to Apollos, Paul, and the Corinthians (3:1–4:21)

Given the argument of 1:17b–2:16, how then should the Corinthians view people like Paul, Apollos, Cephas (Peter), or any other gifted preacher or leader?

How should true wisdom shape the self-conception of preachers, both in the ancient world and today? Is the use of elocution or rhetoric inherently wrong? If not, how can we use various communication techniques without contradicting the gospel?

In this section we see that human weakness highlights the power of the Spirit in true gospel proclamation. Paul then redefines the ministerial life of apostolic preaching as one not of ease and continual blessing, but of suffering and hardship. How does he describe the true life and ministry of the apostles (4:8–4:13)? What are some of the implications of this for gospel ministry today? How does this encourage and fuel steadfastness in ministry?

In 4:4–5, Paul describes a clear conscience. He is being accused of lacking true apostolic status because of his suffering. His whole argument turns the tables on such thinking. How does his teaching encourage the suffering pastor, especially one being falsely accused?

Read through the following three sections on *Gospel Glimpses*, *Whole-Bible Connections*, and *Theological Soundings*. Then take time to consider the *Personal Implications* these sections may have for you.

Gospel Glimpses

SUFFERING SERVANTS. Jesus is the ultimate suffering servant of Isaiah 53, but all gospel workers are called to follow a parallel path. True gospel ministry, which is based on true wisdom, will be a suffering ministry. We will look foolish to the world as we live and proclaim the cross. It is our suffering for the name of Christ that actually signifies true success, then. However, the hope of true gospel ministry is the reality of resurrection. The cross, though vital and essential, is not alone in the work of redemption. There is no hope apart from the resurrection (see 1 Corinthians 15). Therefore, while it certainly is a suffering life, the life of gospel ministry is also a hopeful life that looks forward to eternal vindication, blessings, and the only commendation that truly matters: the commendation that comes from God (1 Cor. 4:3–5).

TRUE PREACHING. Given the truth learned in this section, preaching is not an act of rhetorical persuasion. It is a heralding of good news. The two are very different communication acts. In the former, human strength and dynamism are on display. In the latter, Christ crucified is proclaimed, even in the weakness of the preacher. In the faithful proclamation of God's words, the gospel is actually put on display as God's power, by the Spirit, gives new life to sinful people even through a weak and sinful preacher. True preaching is faithfulness to the message; it is an act of trust that God alone can persuade, indeed transform, the listener. Proper listening recognizes God's power and presence in the preacher, and receives the message accordingly.

Whole-Bible Connections

PROPHET AND HERALD. Starting with Adam, God designed the world to be ruled lovingly by his word, and those made in his image were to believe, keep, and speak that word. What was implicit with Adam became explicit with Noah, in that God explicitly told Noah to preach to his generation of the coming judgment of God. From that point forward in Old Testament history, God appointed prophets to speak his word. The prophet's role was simply to present the message. There were to be no emendations or additions. Faithless prophets were severely judged. Faithful prophets were often rejected by men but commended by God. Prophets were to placard the truth, not to manipulate it. Paul, like all believers then and today, was called to faithfully proclaim the good news.

SUFFERING SERVANTS. The story of the Bible is replete with the theme that the cross precedes the crown. This truth is fulfilled in the actual events of Jesus' death on the cross and his resurrection on the third day, but prior to that event and afterward the pattern of the gospel life was the same: suffering is part of following God, but eventual and eternal reward is also the promise for those who follow until the end. In our passage, Paul echoes this principle in order to rebuke and then rebuild the Corinthian conception of the Christian community. When people strive for the crown in this life, disunity erupts. When believers embrace the place of suffering, particularly for the name of Christ, unity is a wonderful by-product.

TRUE WISDOM AND STRENGTH. Along with the principle of the cross before the crown is the nature of true wisdom and strength. God's wisdom is counterintuitive. His definition of strength has always been at odds with that of the world. True wisdom is foolishness to the world. In Genesis 3 we see how Satan undermined and inverted true wisdom by enticing humanity to reject God's word. Ever since, God has been reasserting true wisdom and power, and the predestined death of his Son on the cross was and is the ultimate embodiment of true wisdom. The gospel, as the message of Christ crucified, is the place where true wisdom is found, for in it the power of God is made known.

Theological Soundings

REVELATION. Romans 1 teaches that some things about God can be known through creation—things like his existence, his glory, and his power (Rom. 1:19–20). But this general revelation is not enough to tell us about how salvation is to be found through Jesus Christ. We need what is called special revelation. God has given us that revelation through his Word, the Bible, and he has given us people who proclaim that Word through teaching and preaching. Before the Bible was finalized in its present form, as the canon[2] of Scripture, it was given through prophets; most of it was orally passed down for a time, and all of it was finally written down into books that now comprise the Bible. But it was always clear that God's Word was *his* product and was not to be tampered with. Whether oral or written, God's people were to simply receive it, believe it, and obey it as God's Word.

ILLUMINATION. The Holy Spirit not only inspired the text of Scripture in its initial formation and final form; he also speaks and works through Scripture today. This notion is essential to Paul's argument in this passage. We do not need to worry about using flowery or eloquent words to persuade people, because it is the work of the Spirit to take a biblical sermon and change hearts with it. In fact, highly gifted communicators can get in the way of the authentic work of the Spirit as they speak superficially with moving stories, powerful cadence, and humor. Of course, dull and unprofessional speaking is not helpful either. Rather, the human preacher must constantly prioritize the simple proclamation of the biblical text, with the conviction and confidence that the Holy Spirit will persuade and transform those who hear.

Personal Implications

Take time to reflect on the implications of 1 Corinthians 1:17b–4:21 for your own life today. What did you learn; how have you been shaped; how might you walk more fully in trusting the Lord Jesus? Make notes below on the personal implications for your walk with the Lord of the (1) *Gospel Glimpses*, (2) *Whole-Bible Connections*, (3) *Theological Soundings*, and (4) this passage as a whole.

1. Gospel Glimpses

2. Whole-Bible Connections

3. Theological Soundings

4. 1 Corinthians 1:17b–4:21

▶ **As You Finish This Unit . . .**

Take a moment now to ask for the Lord's blessing and help as you continue in this study of 1 Corinthians. And take a moment also to look back through this unit of study, to reflect on some key things that the Lord may be teaching you—and perhaps to highlight and underline these things to review again in the future.

Definitions

[1] **Rhetoric** – The use of language to communicate effectively.

[2] **Canon** – The list of writings recognized as Scripture, that is, regarded as inspired by God and authoritative in all areas of doctrine and practice. Our OT was already regarded as canonical in Jesus' day. Criteria for NT canonical books include: (1) apostolic authority (Was the book written by or associated with an apostle?); (2) universal acceptance by the church; and (3) unity of message (Is the message of the book consistent with other books recognized as inspired?).

WEEK 5: SEXUAL IMMORALITY AND LEGAL CASES

1 Corinthians 5:1–6:20

The Place of the Passage

Paul has established the theological underpinning of true unity in chapters 1–4. Now he begins an extensive treatment on specific lifestyle issues that are ways in which the Corinthians' current disunity is being expressed. Many of these issues have been reported to Paul, and many may have been posed to Paul in a former letter that has been lost to history. One by one, Paul begins to address these issues, applying the gospel to each circumstance while also giving specific principles and action points. In our immediate section, 5:1–6:20, Paul focuses on an issue of sexual immorality, which involves the principle of the purity of the church, as well as the issue of how local churches should treat legal cases. The issue of adjudicating conflict and immorality in the church in a godly manner is prominent. These two chapters, like the larger section of which they are a part (chs. 5–14), are consistently practical and quite applicable to the church today.

The Big Picture

First Corinthians 5:1–6:20 teaches that the church must maintain its purity in terms of sexuality and in how it deals with strife. In each case, the reality of the church as the body of Christ, holy and Spirit-filled, is the defining vision.

Reflection and Discussion

Read through the complete passage for this study, 1 Corinthians 5:1–6:20. Then review the questions below and write your notes on them concerning this text section, divided into the case of sexual immorality within a family (5:1–13), the issue of legal cases among believers (6:1–11), and sexual immorality regarding prostitutes (6:12–20). (For further background, see the *ESV Study Bible*, pages 2197–2199, or visit www.esvbible.org.)

1. Incest, arrogance, and the need for discipline (5:1–13)

Paul says that his judgment with regard to a man living in sexual sin with his father's wife (i.e., his stepmother) is true and authoritative in that his spirit, along with the power and the name of Jesus, are authoritative pronouncements in this case of incest (vv. 3–5). Do pastors or other Christians have that kind of authority today? If not, what basis does the church have for church discipline?

What is at stake in church discipline, according to Paul? When someone comes under church discipline and has to be excommunicated, what is the purpose of that excommunication?[1]

Paul speaks of the difference between a believer living in unrepented sin and an unbeliever who lives in sin. What is the difference, and how does that affect our approach to and fellowship with each?

2. Trivial cases before unrighteous judges (6:1–11)

There seem to be cases of fraud and property rights violations within the Corinthian church community, and some of the believers are suing each other in the secular court system. What theological reasons does Paul give here for why believers should adjudicate such matters within the church rather than in civil courts?

Does this section mean that believers should never use secular courts? If there is room for believers to use secular courts, how might the principles in this text be used to create a godly process?

First Corinthians 6:9–11 is a transitional section, coming off of 6:1–8 and anticipating the themes of 6:12–20. Paul reminds the church that unrighteous people will not inherit the kingdom of God: they are not members of the kingdom, nor will they share in its eternal reward. Paul then lists several sinful lifestyles characteristic of the unrighteous person. Does this list suggest that anyone who struggles with such things will not be received by Jesus and have entrance into heaven? What verse in this passage teaches that simply struggling with such sins does not cut us off from grace? So, how would you characterize the person represented in verses 9–10?

3. Sexual immorality and the body's resurrection (6:12–20)

In 1 Corinthians 6:12, as in 10:23, Paul seems to be quoting a well-known slogan on permissibility: "all things are lawful for me." Paul then counters with his own statement that "not all things are helpful." The point is that the gospel does not give free permission to live in sin. Paul then gives a theologically rich vision of the body. How does he describe the human body in terms of Jesus? The Spirit? The temple? The resurrection also factors into Paul's teaching. How?

In 6:18 Paul teaches that, contrary to much popular teaching today, sexual sin is *not* just like any other sins. How is it that sexual sin is "against" the body while other sins are "outside" the body?

Read through the following three sections on *Gospel Glimpses*, *Whole-Bible Connections*, and *Theological Soundings*. Then take time to consider the *Personal Implications* these sections may have for you.

THE GOSPEL PURIFIES. Although it is a cardinal doctrine that we are saved by grace alone through faith alone in Christ alone, we must not forget that true gospel grace actually transforms us. Thus, in our passage, Paul is very concerned that the Corinthians vigilantly protect and purify their community by confronting and excommunicating an unrepentant sinner, by putting away their contentious lawsuits, and by repenting of their sexual sin with cult prostitutes and any other form of sex outside of marriage. In other words, moral permissiveness is not grace. In fact, the unity of the body of Christ is cultivated by godly purity maintained through church discipline.

RESTORATION. Along with healthy church discipline, the restoration of repentant sinners is essential. Church discipline is not punitive but rather is redemptive. Sinners, if unrepentant, are to be confronted and even excommunicated, in order that they may come to realize the horrific nature of their sins (5:5). Removing an unrepentant sinner from Christian fellowship is meant either to reveal an actual state of unbelief or to bring the offender to the end of himself, so that he comes back to Christ in repentance and faith. This fusion of purity and redemption is a gospel balance that many churches need to re-embrace.

IDOLATRY AND SEXUAL SIN. Concerning sexual sin, there is a consistent theme running through the Old and New Testaments: idolatry always leads to sexual sin. Indeed, sexual aberrations were a central part of ancient pagan religions. And it is true in our day as well: where there are impure beliefs, there are impure lives. Paul makes a radical point related to this, in 1 Corinthians 6:18–20: sexual sin is within the body, even though the body of a believer is to be "a temple of the Holy Spirit" (v. 19). The temple is the place of worship, where the holy presence of God dwells, where worship is expressed. Therefore, when it is found that there is sexual sin in a believer's life, the first issue to address is not the sexual sin itself but the idols and false worship that have drawn the believer away from God.

THE HOLY PRESENCE OF GOD. The idea of a temple goes back to the garden of Eden, where the Genesis description of the garden represents a four-sided expanse, with an east-facing entrance and two "images of God" within it— Adam and Eve (Gen. 1:27). The theme of the temple unfolds thenceforth, culminating in Solomon's temple in the Old Testament. However, even Solomon's temple was not the ultimate reality of the temple. In John 2 Jesus says that *he* is the temple, and as the true temple, all access to and worship of God must occur through him. And it does not stop there. In the letters of the New Testament, we see a further application. The *church* is the temple of the Holy Spirit (Ephesians 2), and each *individual believer* is a mini-temple (1 Cor. 6:19). Thus worship, holiness, and reverential respect of human sexual purity are all part of finding our place in God's presence, within his holy temple.

Theological Soundings

HOLINESS. God's presence demands holiness, for he is holy. The issue of sanctification (v. 11) is based on this notion of holiness. The holiness of God is what drives the purity of the church. Those who call upon God and bear his name must strive for holiness, both in terms of their own bodies, which are temples of the Holy Spirit, and in terms of the community as a whole—which may require excommunicating people from time to time. Sometimes, a church's efforts to protect its holiness may seem harsh or judgmental, but usually that perception occurs among those who do not fully appreciate the holiness of God himself. The church is called out from the world, set apart, meant to reflect the holiness of God.

UNION OF BODY AND SPIRIT. The human body is not simply material; it is also a spiritual reality. Body and spirit can never be separated. To be in the image of God, then, is to share in God's spirituality. That does not mean we are a part of God. We are distinct from him. Yet we reflect the spiritual union of matter and spirit. That is why sexual sin is so powerful. It not only injures us thoroughly; it also injures our relationship with God in devastating ways. As Paul says in 1 Corinthians 6:16–17, the union we have with another in sex and the union we have with the Lord are inextricably bound. When someone has sex outside of marriage, it is not merely a material dysfunction but a spiritual act of idolatry and misplaced worship.

Personal Implications

Take time to reflect on the implications of 1 Corinthians 5:1–6:20 for your own life today. What did you learn; how have you been shaped; how might you walk more fully trusting the Lord Jesus? Make notes below on the personal implications for your walk with the Lord of the (1) *Gospel Glimpses*, (2) *Whole-Bible Connections*, (3) *Theological Soundings*, and (4) this passage as a whole.

1. Gospel Glimpses

2. Whole-Bible Connections

3. Theological Soundings

4. 1 Corinthians 5:1–6:20

As You Finish This Unit . . .

Take a moment now to ask for the Lord's blessing and help as you continue in this study of 1 Corinthians. And take a moment also to look back through this unit of study, to reflect on some key things that the Lord may be teaching you—and perhaps to highlight and underline these things to review again in the future.

Definitions

[1] **Excommunication** – In the NT, a form of church discipline that revoked a person's privileges as part of the community of believers. Typically imposed for unrepented sin or heresy, to preserve the community's purity and hopefully to bring the offender to repentance (Matt. 18:15–18; 1 Corinthians 5; 2 Cor. 2:5–11; 1 Tim. 1:18–20).

Week 6: Questions and Answers, Part 1: Marriage, Divorce, Betrothal, Widows

1 Corinthians 7:1–40

▲

First Corinthians 7:1–40 continues an extended discussion of practical Christian living, now in response to questions previously submitted in a letter to Paul (7:1). It is part of a larger section, 7:1–11:1, which handles several overriding issues of marriage, divorce, singleness, food offered to idols, and other matters of Christian identity and lifestyle. The historical background is that of a Gentile Christian church, whose members formerly lived as pagans did. Their view of marriage, sexuality, singleness, divorce, and children, and their former status in terms of ethnicity, vocation, and paganism all come into play. Thus, another key question Paul responds to is, what changed when I became a Christian, and what does that mean for what stays the same and what needs to be left behind?

The Big Picture

First Corinthians 7:1–40 teaches that our identity is most fundamentally in Christ, rather than in our circumstances of marriage, singleness, vocation, and ethnicity.

> ## Reflection and Discussion

Read through the complete passage for this study, 1 Corinthians 7:1–40. Then review the questions below and write your notes on them concerning this larger section, broken down into the issues of marriage, divorce, and unchangeable circumstances (7:1–24), and betrothal and widows (7:25–40). (For further background, see the *ESV Study Bible*, pages 2199–2202, or visit www.esvbible.org.).

1. Marriage, divorce, and unchangeable circumstances (7:1–24)

Paul begins this section by addressing a question about the goodness of sexuality (vv. 1–5). He affirms its goodness within marriage and in fact suggests that sexual relations be a regular part of marriage. What is his condition for times of abstinence within marriage? What does Paul mean by saying that the husband and wife have authority over each other's body?

The validity and even priority of remaining unmarried is a strong theme in our text. How do we square this with the other teachings of Scripture, such as the creation account in Genesis, that present marriage as a wonderful and even assumed circumstance for most men and women? Paul offers a qualification to his recommendation to remain single. What is it?

Divorce is a controversial topic. It is never a good thing, but Paul gives some conditions for divorce here. Look up some of the teachings of Jesus in the Gospels on this topic (Matt. 5:32; 19:9; Mark 10:11–12; Luke 16:18). How does Paul add to or further explain the conditions for divorce?

Paul is not teaching that one should begin an ungodly lifestyle, or enter into a status not pleasing to God, after conversion. But he is teaching that, if one is converted while living in a circumstance that is not ideal yet is redeemable— such as marriage to an unbeliever, or slavery—one does not necessarily need to change that status. How do we know what kinds of life patterns must be repented of by new believers, and what kinds may be allowed to continue, even though they are less than God's ideal for us?

2. The betrothed and widows (7:25–40)

Paul speaks of the "present distress" (v. 26). How does Paul envision the days in which the Corinthian church lived? Look at texts such as 1 Thessalonians 5:1–9 to help you understand Paul's views on the final days. Also, read Jesus' teaching in Matthew 24:36–51; Mark 13:32–37; Luke 17:26–30.

What reasons does Paul give for choosing to remain unmarried? Do these reasons square with the reasons many young people today choose to avoid or delay marriage? If married, is it impossible to be single-minded about the Lord? If it is possible, how specifically might married people be fully committed to their spouse and yet live with gospel urgency in these final days?

In the Old Testament, singleness was a curse. In fact, for a woman to be single (and thus unable to have children) was for her to be in an "afflicted" status (e.g., 1 Sam. 1:11). What has changed in the new covenant? Is there any notion in the New Testament that marriage and procreation have been lowered in status?

Read through the following three sections on *Gospel Glimpses*, *Whole-Bible Connections*, and *Theological Soundings*. Then take time to consider the *Personal Implications* these sections may have for you.

Gospel Glimpses

THE GOSPEL CHANGES EVERYTHING. When someone becomes regenerated by the Holy Spirit, everything changes. But *how* the gospel changes everything involves important nuances. According to our text, not every outward circumstance must change or should change. Certain things *must* change, such as sexual practices, what one worships, how one treats other people, and many other things that are essential moral characteristics. Yet circumstances such as marital status, the presence or absence of circumcision, or one's vocation do not necessarily need to be negated or changed. But everything does change in some regard, and usually significantly. From action to attitude, the gospel gives us a fundamentally new understanding of life.

THE DIGNITY OF SINGLENESS. Marriage was a blessing in Old Testament times, while singleness and barrenness were a curse. The book of Ruth shows this reality. But with the coming of Christ and the establishment of his kingdom, while marriage and procreation are still a means of multiplying God's people, this happens even more essentially through evangelization and discipleship. Paul can, therefore, commend singleness not only as an option but as a preferable one, for single people can be free to give their full devotion to God and his kingdom.

Whole-Bible Connections

MARRIAGE AND COVENANT. It is not coincidental that the first human relationship in the Bible is a marriage between Adam and Eve. The image of God is expressed in this relationship, as is the very identity of the triune[1] God (see Gen. 1:26–28). As the Bible unfolds, it becomes clearer that marriage represents in large part God's covenant with his people. This covenant is one marked by love and promise. So, while marriage is indeed about the love and promise between husband and wife, its ultimate meaning is found in how it reflects God's promises and commitment to us, his people. Our text assumes and reflects this whole-Bible theology as it shows the depth of commitment that marriage requires and thus the cost one needs to count before one enters into marriage.

THE TIME HAS GROWN SHORT. The Bible has always had a time-oriented direction. There is a lot of pointing forward in biblical stories, types, and prophecies. We have touched on this notion in relation to the "day of the Lord" in our study for Week 2, but it bears some reflection in our present text as well. Paul teaches the Corinthians that they need a new, "war time" mentality. These are not days of casually going about one's business. Rather, these are days that are urgent and brief. Thus, believers need to live with a certain intentionality and intensity. The fact that the world is thus "passing away" (1 Cor. 7:31) does not mean that everyone must take the exact same course on questions such as whether to marry or not, but it does mean that we must have a "travel light" mind-set, so that all of our life-decisions take into account our longing to be single-minded toward the Lord in these final, ultimately brief days.

Theological Soundings

HOLINESS. God is completely "other." He is utterly distinct and set apart. That is what holiness means. As his people, we are now set apart as well. We are distinct from the people who belong to and are identified by the world.

There is a moral component to all of this, but the fundamental meaning of holiness is that we are identified with God and therefore distinct from the world. In our text we see this doctrine applied to the spouse of a believer as well as the children of that union (vv. 12–16). Because of the radical nature of the spiritual union that exists between a husband and wife, if one of them becomes a Christian, and thus becomes holy in Christ, this status in some way covers the marriage as well, and it even covers the children of that marriage. This is not to say that the unbelieving spouse or child automatically receives the benefits of grace. It simply indicates that the marriage, and therefore the family, is set apart in its social and formal aspect. Lord willing, the unbelieving spouse and the children too will come to faith and thus be spiritually set apart as well.

CHRIST, THE BRIDEGROOM. In Revelation 19 John gives a vision of the church's future. We will be wed to Jesus Christ, the Lamb of God, and there will be great rejoicing, feasting, and celebration. In Ephesians 5 Paul uses the imagery of the ultimate marriage between Christ and the church to explain what human marriage is all about. The Lord is ours, and we are his. Because this is what marriage signifies, ultimately, and the post-Pentecost ministry of Christ reveals this truth to the ages, Paul is free to recommend singleness as a beneficial life calling. Single Christians are in fact walking sermons attesting to the truth that one day we will all be wholly joined to Christ, in his heavenly kingdom, forever. This heavenly marriage is a truth that should enrapture the believer. It is one of the most wondrous gifts of the gospel.

▶ Personal Implications

Take time to reflect on the implications of 1 Corinthians 7:1–40 for your own life today. What did you learn; how have you been shaped; how might you walk more fully trusting the Lord Jesus? Make notes below on the personal implications for your walk with the Lord of the (1) *Gospel Glimpses*, (2) *Whole-Bible Connections*, (3) *Theological Soundings*, and (4) this passage as a whole.

1. Gospel Glimpses

2. Whole-Bible Connections

3. Theological Soundings

4. 1 Corinthians 7:1–40

As You Finish This Unit . . .

Take a moment now to ask for the Lord's blessing and help as you continue in this study of 1 Corinthians. And take a moment also to look back through this unit of study, to reflect on some key things that the Lord may be teaching you—and perhaps to highlight and underline these things to review again in the future.

Definitions

[1] **Triune** – The Godhead exists in three distinct persons: Father, Son, and Holy Spirit. There is one God, yet he is three persons; there are not three Gods, nor do the three persons merely represent different aspects or modes of a single God. While the term "Trinity" is not found in the Bible, the concept is repeatedly assumed and affirmed by the writers of our NT (e.g., Matt. 28:19; Luke 1:35; 3:22; Gal. 4:6; 2 Thess. 2:13–14; Heb. 10:29).

WEEK 7: QUESTIONS AND ANSWERS, PART 2: FOOD AND IDOLATRY

1 Corinthians 8:1–11:1

▲

The Place of the Passage

Although 1 Corinthians 8:1–11:1 is a subsection of three issues raised in a previous letter that Paul is now responding to (7:1–11:1), it is a lengthy response and deserves its own chapter in our study. The presenting issue of this passage is how Christians ought to handle meat that has been sacrificed to idols in pagan religious services. The underlying principle is that Christians should use their freedoms and rights to the advantage of others, not themselves. While Paul teaches that meat sacrificed to an idol is not inherently tainted, he also teaches that participating in an actual pagan temple ceremony is sinful (10:6–22). Therefore, there are important moral differences among various situations. Some situations are open to various applications while others involve clearer moral issues.

The Big Picture

1 Corinthians 8:1–11:1 unpacks how God-honoring decisions need to be made in controversial situations that require the balance of biblical freedom, cultural awareness, and love for other believers.

> ## Reflection and Discussion

Read through the complete passage for this study, 1 Corinthians 8:1–11:1. Then review the shorter sections below and write your own notes concerning this passage, which we will break into three units: meat sacrificed to idols (8:1–13), the principle of sacrifice (9:1–27), fleeing idolatry (10:1–22), and seeking the glory of God (10:23–11:1). (For further background, see the *ESV Study Bible*, pages 2202–2206, or visit www.esvbible.org.)

1. Meat sacrificed to idols (8:1–13)

Paul shifts the focus in the question-and-answer section of 1 Corinthians to the issue of meat sacrificed to idols (8:1). "Knowledge" is a key word in this chapter. How does our knowledge of the effect of our decisions on other Christians impinge on our choices?

If there is only one true God, why is the issue of idol worship so powerful in the Corinthian context? What are some contemporary issues similar to the issue of meat sacrificed to idols in New Testament times?

2. The principle of sacrifice (9:1–27)

What does it mean for the Corinthians to be Paul's "workmanship" and the "seal" of his apostleship in the Lord (9:1–2)? If Paul is an apostle and therefore has the rights of authority and is entitled to many benefits, why does he give up those rights?

In 9:16, Paul speaks of boasting. In what way is this kind of boasting commendable? If we should give up certain earthly rewards for the sake of ministry, what is the true reward we await (v. 18)?

First Corinthians 9:19–23 is cited often in relation to doing missionary ministry in such a way that we adapt appropriately to our host culture, a process called contextualization. What are some lines that believers should never cross in our desire to contextualize to a host culture? In verses 24–27, how do the athletic images Paul portrays help us understand what our attitude should be in the use of rights, sacrifice, and ministry?

3. Fleeing idolatry, seeking the glory of God (10:1–11:1)

Paul's tone shifts as he forbids participation in meals that are actually part of a pagan worship ceremony (10:7). How does this context change the situation, making it more clear-cut morally?

What is the Old Testament narrative Paul uses as a primary theological grid to explain his point in 10:1–13? How might the Corinthians be playing with fire, so to speak, by using their "freedom" to actually sit and eat amid a pagan ceremony?

How are the glory of God and the good of others connected in 10:31–33?

Read through the following three sections on *Gospel Glimpses*, *Whole-Bible Connections*, and *Theological Soundings*. Then take time to consider the *Personal Implications* these sections may have for you.

> ## Gospel Glimpses

SELF DISADVANTAGE. There is no more powerful expression of the love of God than the cross. The cross is where Jesus emptied himself of his infinite rights and glory for our salvation and thus where he himself experienced joy and ironic glory (Phil. 2:6–11; Heb. 12:1–3). This pattern is essential to the Christian life, and Paul dips into that very theological pool to make his point about the use of Christian liberty: "Let no one seek his own good, but the good of his neighbor" (1 Cor. 10:24). We are to "disadvantage" ourselves for the advantage of others, and if this means we are constantly sacrificing rights that are clearly ours, then that is not only fair but also deeply meaningful, because in this action the gospel itself is displayed.

GOSPEL PATIENCE AND PROTECTIVENESS. Along with the call to disadvantage ourselves for the advantage of our brothers and sisters in Christ, we are to be driven by Christlike patience and protectiveness toward those who are less mature in the faith or in their theological understanding and who therefore are more easily burdened by matters of Christian liberty. Certain items, such as alcohol, have cultural attachments. Many believers have been saved out of debauched backgrounds that involved alcohol abuse, and their new life in Christ means freedom from that addiction. At times those believers assign a moral significance to parts of their past that were not inherently immoral, rather than viewing it as misuse or overuse of something potentially good. The gospel calls us to love such people, not by first setting them straight theologically but by being patient and protecting their weaker conscience by sacrificing our right to do something or participate in something that might be a burden to them. As Christians, not all of our rights are inalienable. Each right is a gift of grace and, in that sense, not a right but a privilege.

> ## Whole-Bible Connections

IDOLATRY. Idolatry can be defined, within an overarching understanding of what sin is, as misplaced trust in something other than the one true God. Whereas, literally, idolatry is the manipulation of a man-made representation of a god for the purpose of religious observance, the presenting issue of our passage is Hellenistic[1] pagan rituals involving animal sacrifices. Throughout the Bible, a significant part of the overarching storyline is idolatry. Idolatry was at the heart of Jewish legalism, in that the law of God, and the human control and merit involved in legalism, became a replacement for God himself. How are we to protect ourselves from idolatry? Paul commends two approaches: One, realize that an idol is nothing; there is only one true God. Two, be humble; pride goes before a fall, and those who are proud exhibit the heart conditions that feed idolatry.

TRUE LIBERTY. Liberty is a misunderstood idea, especially among democratic societies. Liberty is often defined as autonomy and the free exercise of choice. But biblical freedom has always been defined as the mark of a godly person who joyfully submits to the rule of God, as evidenced in God-centered service to others. Jesus expressed freedom ultimately when he chose to give himself on the cross for our salvation. In Galatians, a letter focusing on the true freedom found in the gospel, freedom is defined not as autonomy but as faith working through love (Gal. 5:6). This principle of freedom is at the heart of how Christians should use their "freedoms" to bless others, not to burden or trip them up.

▶ Theological Soundings

INCARNATION. The doctrine of the incarnation states that God sent his Son to take on flesh, in order to reveal God, to represent sinful humanity under God's judgment, and to thus deal with sin as Savior and Lord. The incarnation plays two significant roles in our passage: First, the truth that God sent his Son to take on flesh means that our hunger to have a visible expression of the invisible and transcendent God is fulfilled in Jesus. We no longer need to ask God to reveal himself, or to make himself known, for he has fully revealed himself in Jesus Christ (Col. 1:15–20). Second, idolatry is not compatible with biblical faith. Syncretism never works. False worship leads away from God to destruction, and so idolatry must be something we flee from whenever we encounter it.

▶ Personal Implications

Take time to reflect on the implications of 1 Corinthians 8:1–11:1 for your own life today. What did you learn; how have you been shaped; how might you walk more fully trusting the Lord Jesus? Make notes below on the personal implications for your walk with the Lord of the (1) *Gospel Glimpses*, (2) *Whole-Bible Connections*, (3) *Theological Soundings*, and (4) this passage as a whole.

1. Gospel Glimpses

2. Whole-Bible Connections

3. Theological Soundings

4. 1 Corinthians 8:1–11:1

As You Finish This Unit . . .

Take a moment now to ask for the Lord's blessing and help as you continue in this study of 1 Corinthians. And take a moment also to look back through this unit of study, to reflect on some key things that the Lord may be teaching you—and perhaps to highlight and underline these things to review again in the future.

Definitions

[1] **Hellenism** – A modified form of Greek culture, philosophy, religion, politics, and language that was spread throughout the Mediterranean world by the exploits of Alexander the Great. Hellenism continued to have great influence throughout the time of the Roman empire.

Week 8: Glory, Unity, and Worship Order

1 Corinthians 11:2–16

▲

Having addressed some practical ethical matters, Paul now turns his attention to three areas in which the Corinthian church is not living according to God's will regarding gathered worship. The issue of immediate concern in our passage is head coverings in worship, and yet the fundamental issue is really about how God's glory is expressed through the visible deportment of husbands and wives in the public worship gatherings of a local church, which in turn reflects the relationship between God the Father and God the Son. The letter's three primary themes of speech, knowledge, and spiritual gifts become more prominent throughout these chapters. At first glance, the issue of head coverings does not seem very relevant to the church in our day, but this is a good example of how to recognize and distinguish between abiding theological principles and mere culturally bound applications.

> ## The Big Picture

First Corinthians 11:2–16 explains how the relationship between God the Father and God the Son is reflected in the deportment of husbands and wives within the gathered worship of a local church in the first century.

> ## Reflection and Discussion

Read through the complete passage for this study, 1 Corinthians 11:2–16. Then review the questions below and write your notes on them. (For further background, see the *ESV Study Bible*, pages 2206–2207, or visit www.esvbible.org.)

1. Head coverings and worship (11:2–16)

Paul's argument in these verses can be confusing at first. Try and carefully map out the relationships involved here, between God the Father and God the Son, and then between husbands and wives. How does Paul speak of each relationship? How does Genesis 1 speak of the image of God and humanity, and how does that relate to our passage?

In the historical context of New Testament times, to drape a shawl or other piece of cloth over a man was to mimic how men worshiped in pagan rituals (see our previous chapter, about fleeing idolatry). But for a woman to have a head covering was a sign of being married, and of being under her husband's authority. It is similar to the symbol of a wedding ring today. This helps us understand that Paul is speaking here of married couples, not of men and women in general. With that in mind, why is it important that Paul talks about husbands and wives and the nature of head coverings? What is at stake theologically in this issue?

Authority is a central idea in our passage. How does the relationship between the Father and the Son within the Trinity help us understand that individuals may have different roles but equal worth?

Note that Paul begins this section by commending the Corinthians (11:2). It may be that they were faithfully adhering to the external ritual of head coverings for women while not fully understanding why they should do so; or perhaps they were doing so with wrong motives. How does the contemporary church superficially carry out right worship without necessarily having the right heart or theology behind it? How can we remain healthy not just in our external forms but also in our underlying motives?

Read through the following three sections on *Gospel Glimpses*, *Whole-Bible Connections*, and *Theological Soundings*. Then take time to consider the *Personal Implications* these sections may have for you.

Gospel Glimpses

DIGNITY IN SUBMISSION. The principles of this passage reflect many of the explicit ideas Paul teaches in Ephesians 5:22–33. Our contemporary world, especially those societies premised on egalitarian ideals, struggles with the idea of headship and submission and often relegates it to an ancient and outmoded form of thinking. Yet in the gospel, submission is dignified, even glorious. Thus, when a wife aligns herself with her husband, however that might look today—perhaps with a token of submission in gathered worship—that is not a demeaning gesture but rather a glorious one where her full joy and dignity are actually displayed as she ultimately points to the beauty of God himself.

THE GOSPEL TRANSLATES EVERYWHERE, ALL THE TIME. At first glance, this passage might seem irrelevant, but it is not. The cultural symbols of head coverings, hair length for each gender, and even how clothing has imaging power, may not translate to our modern world in the same way, but the principles here are timeless—otherwise this passage is like an ancient artifact, interesting but no longer relevant. But all Scripture is relevant and timeless. The principles of the Bible are gospel-based truths. The gospel is always meant to be embodied in our practices, and so it is incumbent upon us to pray and discern what it means for us to apply these timeless principles.

Whole-Bible Connections

RIGHT WORSHIP. There is a consistent pattern in the Bible with regards to Israel's spiritual health being expressed in how they understood their worship. When Israel was seeking the Lord, they took worship seriously, and this was evident in how meticulously and yet affectionately they kept God's word with regard to the sacrifices, the role of the priests, and the centrality of the Scriptures. When Israel was beset by idolatry and pride, they forsook biblical worship and self-righteously carried out the externals of worship, attempted syncretistic[1] forms of worship, or simply replaced scriptural worship with the worship of the pagan cultures around them—such as Baalism. The bottom line was always the question of whether God would be at the center of worship, and at the center of the heart of the worshiper. The question remains for us today.

Theological Soundings

THE TRIUNE RELATIONSHIP. Although the Trinity is notoriously difficult to define in human terms, the triune God is ever present, ever at work, and ever Father, Son, and Spirit, both in the Scriptures and in the realm of reality. The language of the three persons is most explicit in the New Testament, and there we begin to see the nuances of the relationship between the persons of the Godhead. First Corinthians 11:2–16 is a good example of a passage that describes the relationship between the Father and the Son. Verse 3 says that the Father is the "head of," or authority over, the Son. This reflects several other passages, especially in the Gospel of John, where Jesus claims this very thing (John 5:19; 14:28). Though the Father, Son, and Holy Spirit are equal in every way, they are unique persons with unique roles. This is a paradox, but a reality nonetheless.

HUMANITY AND GENDER. God has designed what it means to be human with a purpose and with meaningful order. In the beginning God made mankind to be "in his own image" (Gen. 1:27). With that image came a call (Gen. 1:28–31). There is a fundamental and unchangeable link between the image and the call, and our theology of humanity must respect that linkage. In Genesis 1, the first description of what it means to be human is that we are made by God, for God, as two genders. Our genders are thus not man-made, pragmatic, or culturally bound. To be male or to be female is a fixed reality, with a purpose for each gender. One of the most important implications of this is that the genders are to be binary complements in sexuality, with no other option. All the Old Testament and New Testament sexual ethics reflect this. Another implication, related to this, is that we are to conform to our genders, to our given fundamental characteristics of masculinity and femininity, and to the cultural norms for us today (see Deut. 22:5).

Personal Implications

Take time to reflect on the implications of 1 Corinthians 11:2–16 for your own life today. What did you learn; how have you been shaped; how might you walk more fully trusting the Lord Jesus? Make notes below on the personal implications for your walk with the Lord of the (1) *Gospel Glimpses*, (2) *Whole-Bible Connections*, (3) *Theological Soundings*, and (4) this passage as a whole.

1. Gospel Glimpses

2. Whole-Bible Connections

3. Theological Soundings

4. 1 Corinthians 11:2–16

Take a moment now to ask for the Lord's blessing and help as you continue in this study of 1 Corinthians. And take a moment also to look back through this unit of study, to reflect on some key things that the Lord may be teaching you—and perhaps to highlight and underline these things to review again in the future.

Definitions

[1] **Syncretism** – The creation of a new religious system by blending together ideas and practices of various religions.

Week 9: Love, Unity, and Worship Order

1 Corinthians 11:17–14:40

The Place of the Passage

Paul has just addressed the issue of head coverings in worship, and he now turns his attention to two other issues related to gathered worship: the Lord's Supper and spiritual gifts. This longer section has the theme of unity front and center, and thus is a climactic exhortation in this letter. These chapters are being kept together in this study because the theme of unity is so clear and so powerfully connected to the issues at hand, as well as because this passage begins a new argument in which Paul is responding to a specific scandal reported to him. Perhaps the most fundamental section of the entire letter resides in our passage, namely, 1 Corinthians 13, the love chapter. One may view chapter 13 as the core of our section, and of the entire letter. In this section it serves as a bridge between two chapters on the use of spiritual gifts in worship—chapters 12 and 14.

The Big Picture

First Corinthians 11:17–14:40 teaches that loving unity is paramount in the church's life, especially in the context of the Lord's Supper and in the use of spiritual gifts. The sign of love is that all things are done in proper relationship to the reality of the gospel and for the building up of other Christians.

> ### Reflection and Discussion

Read through the complete passage for this study, 1 Corinthians 11:17–14:40. Then review the questions below and write your notes on them. This section will be broken up into three parts: social snobbery and the Lord's Supper (11:17–34), elevating one spiritual gift above others (12:1–31 and 14:1–40), and the way of love (13:1–13). (For further background, see the *ESV Study Bible*, pages 2207–2213, or visit www.esvbible.org.)

1. Social snobbery at the Lord's Supper (11:17–34)

The subject at hand is the Lord's Supper. It is likely that the Corinthian church assembled in a large home, and that this church was made up of financially and socially elite as well as working-class or economically poorer believers. The Lord's Supper may have been a full meal, and as was the custom of the day, the rich would have been served first, then the poor. The rich were eating the entirety of the meal, leaving the poor with little to nothing (11:20–21). How does such an action work against the very reality to which the meal is intended to point?

The assumption behind Paul's rebuke is that the Lord's Supper has significant horizontal implications. The meal should involve not only divine communion but also communion of believers together. How does this help you understand what Paul says in 11:22–29?

In verse 30, Paul speaks of physical judgments as a result of ungodly worship. How do we understand the relationship between disobedience and physical judgment (look at 5:5 for context)?

2. Elevating one spiritual gift above others (12:1–31 and 14:1–40)

In these two chapters, what are the gifts with which the Spirit empowers believers? For what purpose?

In 12:12–30 Paul uses the metaphor of the human body to explain the reality of spiritual gifts in the church. How does that metaphor contribute to our understanding of the diversity, unity, and equality of people and their gifts? What happens if everyone wants to be a head, like the Corinthians? What happens, on the other hand, if there are only "unpresentable" parts and no "more presentable" ones (vv. 23–24)?

In chapter 14, what is the gift that seems to be getting top billing? Why might it be tempting to elevate such a gift?

There is controversy over whether certain gifts mentioned in this section still exist today. The gifts usually in question are tongues, prophecy, and healing. Study the passage alongside other related passages, such as Acts 2 and the lists of spiritual gifts in Ephesians 4:1–16 and Romans 12:3–8. Regardless of your convictions on these gifts for today, draw out some principles you see in our passage on the use of these visible and powerful gifts.

The principles of clarity and intelligibility are central in 1 Corinthians 14. How is evangelism, in particular, tied to intelligibility in 14:24–25? What are some questions we should always ask as we design our worship services?

3. The way of love (13:1–13)

First Corinthians 13 is so important that we have given it its own section. Given the context, what kind of love is Paul talking about?

Biblical love may be defined as faithfulness in word, speech, and action, based on a promise to be kept through grace and solid character. How does this kind of love create unity? In what ways does Paul show the futility that results when there is a lack of such love?

In 13:12, Paul speaks of a "now" versus "then" timeline. What eras of time is he referring to? If he is speaking of "then" as the return of Christ, how does that help us understand whether spiritual gifts such as tongues, prophecy, and healing are relevant for Christians today? Paul concludes with the holy triad of faith, hope, and love. Consider these three virtues and explain why love is the greatest. How does the reality of heaven put faith and hope in a category subordinate to love?

Read through the following three sections on *Gospel Glimpses*, *Whole-Bible Connections*, and *Theological Soundings*. Then take time to consider the *Personal Implications* these sections may have for you.

Gospel Glimpses

GOSPEL COMMUNION. Traditionally, most churches emphasize the need for a repentant heart prior to partaking of the Lord's Supper. This is of course part of rightly taking the elements, which represent the broken body and shed blood of Jesus for our sins—but there is more to it. In our passage, the main issue is the relationships within the Corinthian church, as social snobbery has crept in, and Paul cites the Upper Room Discourse as the theological basis for saying that their behavior is a misappropriation of the meal. Paul is teaching that Christ's work on the cross not only heals our vertical relationship with God; it also binds believers together into a new family. The church should reflect this wonderful reality as it comes together for this beautiful act of worship.

LOVE. "Love" is a slippery word. For the most part, in our contemporary world, "love" means an emotion tantamount to a crush. It tends to be based on reciprocation and self-esteem, and is quite fleeting. But love is central to the gospel and therefore must be central to the church. And it must be biblically understood. The Corinthian church had lost track of love. That was its fundamental problem. The Corinthians were good at lusting, envying, competing, and disdaining, but they were not so good at loving. To sum it up succinctly, if the Corinthians would simply fill their minds and hearts with the gospel, then they would understand love. If they understood love, then they would love each other well. This, in turn, would create a gospel-unified church and, therefore, a God-glorifying church.

Whole-Bible Connections

THE FULLNESS OF THE SPIRIT. Peter, in his sermon in Acts 2:17–21, cites Joel 2:28–32. The prophet Joel speaks of a coming day when God's Spirit will be poured out upon God's people in full, such that miracles, prophetic words, and clear signs would occur, signifying that the day of the Lord was coming. One of the most important elements of that final day is the bestowing of the Spirit in fullness. Though the Corinthian church was misappropriating the power of the Spirit due to pride, the fact that they were gifted with the Spirit is good news, signifying that they were living in the final days of God's work.

MIRACLES. There is controversy about how to define the miraculous gifts Paul mentions in our passage—tongues, prophecy, and healing—and whether these gifts are still operative for the church today. And, if they are still operative, should we expect them to be a regular part of our Christian experience? Our present study does not afford the scope or time to navigate these issues, and it will be left to the reader to delve more fully into them. However, there are some biblical patterns that all Bible-believing Christians can agree upon: First, miracles happen because God is sovereign and is the sustainer of all things at every moment. Second, miracles serve to prove that God exists and that he is the true God among a host of competing powers (see the Exodus narrative). Third, when God uses human servants to show his power, miracles serve to authenticate the servant as having been sent by God. And fourth, miracles tend to cluster around key individuals and decisive moments in biblical history. Whether or not the Spirit still gives ongoing gifts of tongues, prophecy, or healing to individuals today, miracles do occur.

Theological Soundings

SACRAMENT/ORDINANCE. Protestant evangelicals hold that there are two acts of worship instituted by Christ that convey the grace of God and help Christians to grow in faith and obedience. They are baptism and the Lord's Supper. Depending on the tradition, these are referred to as either sacraments or ordinances, the former term stressing the actual spiritual presence of Christ in the administration, while the latter stresses the symbolism of the actions. Traditions will vary as to the specifics of how each is applied, from sprinkling to full immersion with baptism, and to the various ways in which the Lord's Supper is celebrated. However, the evangelical consensus is that these two events are vital and biblically commanded, although not necessary for salvation.

GOD THE SPIRIT. God has eternally existed in three persons: Father, Son, and Spirit. The Spirit of God is just as truly God as the other two persons. As we look at the Spirit's actions in the Bible, we see that he manifests the power of God, in the world and in believers, *through* believers. The Bible speaks of him as a seal of salvation (Eph. 1:13), a comforter-helper-strengthener (John 14 and 16), and the giver of gifts (1 Cor. 11:17–14:40). In 1 Corinthians, Paul is focusing on the ministry of the Spirit to empower believers with certain gifts to edify other believers, to add strength to the church, and thus to empower the church for mission and worship.

Personal Implications

Take time to reflect on the implications of 1 Corinthians 11:17–14:40 for your own life today. What did you learn; how have you been shaped; how might you walk more fully trusting the Lord Jesus? Make notes below on the personal implications for your walk with the Lord of the (1) *Gospel Glimpses*, (2) *Whole-Bible Connections*, (3) *Theological Soundings*, and (4) this passage as a whole.

1. Gospel Glimpses

2. Whole-Bible Connections

3. Theological Soundings

4. 1 Corinthians 11:17–14:40

▶ As You Finish This Unit . . .

Take a moment now to ask for the Lord's blessing and help as you continue in this study of 1 Corinthians. And take a moment also to look back through this unit of study, to reflect on some key things that the Lord may be teaching you—and perhaps to highlight and underline these things to review again in the future.

WEEK 10: THE CENTRALITY AND NECESSITY OF THE RESURRECTION

1 Corinthians 15:1–58

The Place of the Passage

Chapter 15 contains Paul's final address regarding a specific issue—a question probably raised by the Corinthians in their previous letter (see 7:1). The issue is the resurrection of the dead. This chapter is key to the whole letter, especially to Paul's teaching in chapters 12–14 on what mature and godly worship looks like, for the truth of the bodily resurrection—that of Jesus foremost, and then that of the believer as a consequence—is the basis for the entire Christian faith. Paul argues that without the resurrection there would be no hope, and the gospel would be a futile and empty message. But with the resurrection, all that he has taught—the reality of the Spirit and the unifying power of the gospel—is true and is at work in the world.

The Big Picture

1 Corinthians 15:1–58 reminds us that the truth of the bodily resurrection of believers in Christ is an essential doctrine for the reality of Christian faith and mission.

▶ Reflection and Discussion

Read through the complete passage for this study, 1 Corinthians 15:1–58. Then review the questions below and write your notes on them. This section will be broken up into three parts: the truthfulness of the traditions about Christ's resurrection (15:1–11); Christ's resurrection and the resurrection of believers (15:12–34); and the nature of the resurrection body (15:35–58). (For further background, see the *ESV Study Bible*, pages 2213–2216, or visit www.esvbible.org.)

1. The truthfulness of the traditions about Christ's resurrection (15:1–11)

Paul reminds the Corinthians that they have received and believed the gospel he preached (15:1, 11). What does that say about their initial response to the teaching of Jesus' resurrection? What does it say about the relationship between initial belief and ongoing faith?

Paul cites several sources of authority for the truth of Jesus' bodily resurrection (15:1–8). What are those sources? If Paul taught the Corinthians about Jesus' death and resurrection "in accordance with the Scriptures," then he is talking about the Old Testament. What are some Old Testament texts that reflect or teach the truth of Christ's resurrection, or resurrection in general?

How does Paul's personal story of conversion legitimize the reality of the resurrection? What does his contrast of "in vain/not in vain" (15:2, 10) contribute to his story?

2. Christ's resurrection and the resurrection of believers (15:12–34).

The Corinthians may have rejected the notion of their own resurrection due to the pressure of Greco-Roman culture, which viewed the post-death experience as ranging from nonexistence to a shadowy and immaterial existence in an underworld. In particular, to an educated person, the idea of a physical and conscious afterlife was thought to be somewhat childish. The Corinthian temptation toward elitism and good breeding was at work again. How is Paul connecting Christ's resurrection to the assurance of resurrection for his disciples?

What does Paul mean by saying that Christ is the "firstfruits" of those who have fallen asleep (15:20, 23)? Paul compares and contrasts Adam and Jesus. How are those two foundational biblical characters alike and how are they different, according to our passage?

If God the Father and God the Son are equal, how can Paul say that Jesus will be in subjection under the Father after the final resurrection (15:28)? What does this teach us about the relationship between the Father and the Son (see also the comments on 11:2–16 in our consideration of "The Triune Relationship" in Week 8)?

A few scenarios that are mentioned in 15:29–34 should motivate the Corinthians to revive their belief in the resurrection. How should belief in the resurrection motivate believers, some of whom may even be killed for their faith (15:31–32)? How should it motivate godly living (15:32b–34)?

3. The nature of the resurrection body (15:35–58)

In this final section, Paul compares the present human body to the future resurrection body. Make a side-by-side list of the two states. Take into account chronology, physicality, the biblical storyline, and eternality. What are some of the ways our current bodies will be transformed after the resurrection?

In 15:54–55, Paul is citing portions of Isaiah 25:8 and Hosea 13:14. How are those texts used in their original contexts, and how is Paul using them to further his case in this passage? What links do you see between these uses?

In verse 58, Paul gives a final exhortation that is a powerful conclusion of his entire argument up to this point. What are the four actions and attitudes the Corinthians should possess as a result of the resurrection?

Read through the following three sections on *Gospel Glimpses*, *Whole-Bible Connections*, and *Theological Soundings*. Then take time to consider the *Personal Implications* these sections may have for you.

▶ Gospel Glimpses

CROSS AND RESURRECTION. Christians should seek to be able to explain the gospel biblically and briefly. The explanation should include God and his creation, the fall, the work of Christ, the new life, and the eternal hope of heaven. Many people can convey these high points well but tend to leave out one very key part of the work of Christ, namely, the resurrection. In other words, the cross gets center stage with hardly a mention of the resurrection. The cross was, of course, the high point of Christ's mission, but without the resurrection it would have been meaningless and ineffective, as our passage teaches. The atoning[1] work of the cross was confirmed by the resurrection.

NEW LIFE. The gospel teaches us the reality of a work that is apart from us, done on our behalf through Jesus, and a reality we cannot change or add to in any measure. This is good news. But the gospel is not merely an objective idea, with no connection to our everyday lives. Rather, the gospel has flesh on it. It actually changes lives, just as Jesus actually became a man and entered into human history. Paul's argument for the reality of the bodily resurrection has massive implications for us in terms of our hope for sanctification, our hope in affliction, and our ability to cope with the aging and deterioration of our mortal bodies.

SUBJECTION AND GLORY. Our contemporary world cannot fathom that two people can be equal in value yet have different roles. If someone has more authority, a higher salary, and has more public acclaim, people tend to put more worth on that person. Yet, in the case of God himself, we see this logic fall apart. In 1 Corinthians 15:28 Paul clearly teaches that, once the work of redemption has been completed and all things are put in subjection to Christ, Christ in turn will give back to the Father all things, including himself, in subjection forever. The Son is functionally subordinate to the Father, even into eternity. The logic of the gospel is such that, if the Father and Son are equal yet have abiding differences in role—including the subordination of the Son to the Father—then how much more in our humanity can we embrace both our equality and our differing roles in life.

Whole-Bible Connections

FIRSTFRUITS. The theme of firstfruits appears throughout the Old Testament, for example, in Exodus 23:19, Leviticus 23:10, and Deuteronomy 18:4. The idea was simple: whatever the Lord gave you by way of material blessing, whether produce, livestock, or other material gain from labor, part of it should be dedicated back to the Lord as a form of worship. This would be the best part, representing the whole of your wealth. When the Bible refers to Jesus as the firstfruits of humanity (1 Cor. 15:20–23), it means that Jesus is the supreme representative of humanity *and* is a sign that the rest of humanity, bound to him in faith, will also share in his status.

DIVINE WARRIOR AND KING. Our passage is fundamentally about resurrection, but another important theme is prominent, that of God as Divine Warrior and King. In the opening chapters of the Bible, a war begins between God and a world ruled by Satan and populated with fallen, rebellious people. The battle begins in Genesis 3, and every part of the storyline that features an earthly battle between God's people and their enemies is but a part of the overall spiritual and heavenly battle God is waging. Paul describes this in Ephesians 6:12: "For we do not wrestle against flesh and blood, but against the rulers, against the authorities, against the cosmic powers over this present darkness, against the spiritual forces of evil in the heavenly places." First Corinthians 15 gives us hope as it promises that God is going to win this battle through his Son, and that one day soon all the world will be conquered and put in subordination under the Son, who will then give it back to the Father.

Theological Soundings

RESURRECTION. The doctrine of the resurrection is stated more clearly and precisely in our passage than in any other passage of Scripture. It is less specific and prominent in the Old Testament, but even there we have clear hints, patterns, and promises that the soul is immortal and that God's people will in some way experience a perfect and everlasting life after physical death. As many truths become clearer and less mysterious after the coming of Christ, the resurrection itself becomes not just more specific but also most prominent. Paul stresses that without the resurrection our faith is in vain (1 Cor. 15:13–14). Thus, the reality of resurrection, first Christ's and then ours, is not a secondary issue but a core truth upon which Christianity rises or falls. The resurrection should be one of the most substantial, frequent, and emphasized teachings of a biblically faithful church, as it speaks of Christ and of our hope of a resurrection like his.

HEAVEN AND ETERNITY. Apart from the death and resurrection of Christ on our behalf, there is probably no more hope-producing truth than the promise of eternal life. The resurrection would not be such a strong and precious hope if it simply meant coming back to life only to eventually die again. No, the resurrection of Jesus Christ means that his eternal body and his eternal existence signal our own. Likewise, the simple notion of eternity would not be that compelling if we were promised merely an unending existence not much different from the present world. Would we really long for that? The Bible promises that our resurrection is sure and will lead to unending life, and that the life we will have will be perfect, transformed to a degree we cannot even fathom, a life with God at the center and with our joy fully engaged in worship and service to God. That is one of the most glorious truths we cling to in this fallen, temporal, and challenging world.

▶ Personal Implications

Take time to reflect on the implications of 1 Corinthians 15:1–58 for your own life today. What did you learn; how have you been shaped; how might you walk more fully trusting the Lord Jesus? Make notes below on the personal implications for your walk with the Lord of the (1) *Gospel Glimpses*, (2) *Whole-Bible Connections*, (3) *Theological Soundings*, and (4) this passage as a whole.

1. Gospel Glimpses

2. Whole-Bible Connections

3. Theological Soundings

4. 1 Corinthians 15:1–58

> ## As You Finish This Unit . . .

Take a moment now to ask for the Lord's blessing and help as you continue in this study of 1 Corinthians. And take a moment also to look back through this unit of study, to reflect on some key things that the Lord may be teaching you—and perhaps to highlight and underline these things to review again in the future.

Definitions

[1] **Atonement** – The reconciliation of a person with God, often associated with the offering of a sacrifice. Through his death and resurrection, Jesus Christ made atonement for the sins of believers. His death satisfied God's just wrath against sinful humanity, just as OT sacrifices symbolized substitutionary death as payment for sin.

Week 11: The Collection for the Saints, Travel Plans, and Farewell Greetings

1 Corinthians 16:1–24

The Place of the Passage

The letter concludes with Paul reminding the Corinthians about an important collection for the needy Jerusalem church (Acts 24:17) and then giving a few updates on his travel plans and finally a brief farewell greeting. The collection for the Jerusalem church was a pointed application of the main theme of 1 Corinthians, for this collection was itself the selfless ministry of a Gentile church to a Jewish church, a beautiful expression of unity around the work of Christ. It was an act of love. Paul had laid out the theological reality of the gospel and how it draws people out of selfishness, pride, elitism, and competitiveness, into a blood-bought unity of those who put their faith and identity in Christ. Even Paul's travel updates assume this unity and love, which are the golden threads of his letter, as he was full of eagerness to see these beloved friends. He ends where he began, with the grace of the Lord Jesus, expressed through his love (1 Cor. 16:23).

The Big Picture

First Corinthians 16:1–24 reveals that gospel unity must be embodied through acts of grace and love, as illustrated here by a collection taken by the Corinthians for the Jerusalem church, by Paul's heartfelt desire to visit with the Corinthians, by the way Paul desires this church to treat other leaders, and by the way Paul encourages this church to press on in faith and mission.

Reflection and Discussion

Read through the complete passage for this study, 1 Corinthians 16:1–24. Then review the questions below and write your notes on them. This section will be broken up into two parts: the collection for the saints and Paul's travel plans (16:1–12), and closing admonitions and greetings (16:13–24). (For further background, see the *ESV Study Bible*, pages 2216–2217, or visit www.esvbible.org.)

1. The collection for the saints and Paul's travel plans (16:1–12)

The letter concludes with a reminder that Paul will be visiting Corinth to collect money for the Jerusalem church. How was the money to be collected (16:1–2)? How would this collection embody the main ideas of this letter?

Paul describes his future travel plans (16:5–9). How does this reveal the heart of a pastor who at times must rebuke his sheep and yet who closes his letter with such words as these?

Paul speaks of a ministry opportunity in Ephesus that compels him to remain there, and yet he adds that there were also many adversaries there (16:8). How is it that both the open door for ministry and the existence of adversaries to the faith are compelling reasons for Paul to stay in a given area?

2. Closing admonitions and greetings (16:13–24)

Paul draws his letter to a close with a farewell admonition, offering five imperatives: "Be watchful, stand firm in the faith, act like men, be strong. Let all that you do be done in love" (16:13–14). How does each of these relate to larger themes in the letter?

Paul encourages the Corinthians to be subject to and give recognition to people like the household of Stephanas and other gospel workers (16:15–18). Given the teaching they had received to this point, how might the Corinthians have had their minds shaped regarding servanthood, subjection, and giving recognition to others?

Look at chapter 1 and this final chapter, and consider: How do the bookends of 1 Corinthians compare to each other? How are tensions resolved? How are themes fulfilled? How is the tone of the two chapters different?

Read through the following three sections on *Gospel Glimpses*, *Whole-Bible Connections*, and *Theological Soundings*. Then take time to consider the *Personal Implications* these sections may have for you.

► Gospel Glimpses

GENTILES SERVE JEWS. At first glance, it may seem that Paul is ending his letter in a formulaic manner, with a few reminders and updates and a standard farewell greeting. Though ancient letters generally may have had these structures, Paul is also ending this letter very pointedly by taking this opportunity to exhort the Corinthians to apply the main idea of the letter: gospel unity. The Corinthian church was fractured within itself due to sinful pride, the entrapments of Greco-Roman bourgeois culture, and superficial theology, and yet we also know from other biblical letters, like Galatians and Ephesians, that there were divisions between Jews and Gentiles. Thus, for Paul to collect money from Gentile churches throughout Asia Minor, including the Corinthian church, was a major testimony to the unifying power of the gospel that could cause two bitter rivals to be joined in a work of mercy and love.

THE MUTUAL LOVE OF LEADERS AND CHURCHES. Paul spoke briefly of the household of Stephanas in 1:16. In this last chapter, Stephanas and his household are referred to again, now in terms of their service to the saints. Paul commands the Corinthians to acknowledge and subject themselves to leaders such as this (16:18). Mutual deference is a fundamental theme of this letter, and now Paul brings it up once again in this exhortation. Leaders should be given authority and recognition so that they can serve those who are subject to them. There should be no power grabs or authoritarianism in the kingdom. The kingdom has leaders, but those leaders lead by serving. When the gospel rules a community, the mutual love of leaders and their people is evident and powerful, and speaks of the work of Jesus for his people.

Whole-Bible Connections

SHALOM AND SERVICE. Ever since the fall of Adam (Genesis 3), the world has experienced a privation of all that it was intended to have, not least in terms of human relationships. Though there are rays of light in the story of the Old Testament, the majority of the historical narratives involve people in conflict. Cain murders Abel (Genesis 4); society breaks down to the point that God must judge the world with a flood (Genesis 6–9); God divides and scatters people throughout the world when they try to build their own godless civilization (Genesis 10–11); and so the story goes. There is disintegration; factions and rivalries abound; and the sexuality that was given to humanity to reflect God's intimacy and love within the covenant of marriage is trivialized, dehumanized, and even used in false worship. Sin creates a world order where people steal life from one another. Yet, in the Old Testament and in our passage, we see how God's reordering of the world through the gospel puts to rights this tragedy. Christ restores love among people who know *his* love.

THE CURSE. Paul uses the last sentences of this letter, written in his own hand (1 Cor. 16:21), quite interestingly. He remarks in verse 22, "If anyone has no love for the Lord, let him be accursed." Then he adds, "Our Lord, come!" Why that line about being accursed? Why not simply end with affection and farewell? Remember, our study has taken us through the reality of the gospel's power to create loving unity based on the work of Christ. The opposite of that, what the Corinthians had unfortunately been allowing in their community, is the power of the curse of sin. As we look to the unfolding plan of the Bible, it was that curse that caused all the dysfunction in the world. And, at root, the curse was the state of being that obscured and rejected the love of God. Paul began with the day of the Lord in 1:7–8, and now we return to it: "Come, Lord!" The curse blinds us to God's love; the gospel wakes us back up to it. The story of the Bible beautifully draws this out, and the promise of Christ's return is a prospect of love that will overflow on all the faithful.

Theological Soundings

ECCLESIOLOGICAL[1] UNITY. There are many ways to think about the ideal life of the church. One can focus on the governance of the church, the role of teaching in the church, the mission of the church, or even how discipline is to be conducted in the church. If there is a particular aspect of the church embedded in our letter, and especially here in chapter 16, it is the unity of the church. Galatians 3:28, one of the best-known texts on the unity of God's people, says, "There is neither Jew nor Greek, there is neither slave nor free, there is no male and female, for you are all one in Christ Jesus." Each of the three pairings in that verse represents two seemingly dichotomous people groups. Paul's point is that the gospel does not just bring good relationship to a level of greatness; the gospel can make former enemies into family members. The doctrine of the unity of the church is one of the more practical doctrines within ecclesiology.

THE RETURN OF CHRIST. In his brief final appeal, in verse 22, Paul uses a common phrase, "Our Lord, Come!" (*Maranatha!*). The day of the Lord was referred to in the opening verses of the letter (1:7–8), and now our attention is drawn back to this grand hope. The Word of God has assured us that not only has Jesus lived a perfect life, died an atoning death, and been raised to glorious life as the firstfruits of salvation; he is also coming back. Paul longed for that day as he expressed his agonized desire that this church would obey his teaching out of love for God; and yet, rather than becoming riddled with unrighteous anxiety or resentment regarding them, he brings himself back to his ultimate hope for his Lord to return to set all things right. The return of Christ is not to be thought of as a far-off and fantastical part of the Christian doctrine of the end times. Our hope in the return of the Lord must underscore our daily lives as a formative force, and it is certainly a backstop and encouragement for pastors who are rightly anxious for their people to love the Lord, obey the Word, and walk in the freedom of the gospel.

Personal Implications

Take time to reflect on the implications of 1 Corinthians 16:1–24 for your own life today. What did you learn; how have you been shaped; how might you walk more fully trusting the Lord Jesus? Make notes below on the personal implications for your walk with the Lord of the (1) *Gospel Glimpses*, (2) *Whole-Bible Connections*, (3) *Theological Soundings*, and (4) this passage as a whole.

1. Gospel Glimpses

2. Whole-Bible Connections

3. Theological Soundings

4. 1 Corinthians 16:1–24

As You Finish This Unit . . .

Take a moment now to ask for the Lord's blessing and help as you continue in this study of 1 Corinthians. And take a moment also to look back through this unit of study, to reflect on some key things that the Lord may be teaching you—and perhaps to highlight and underline these things to review again in the future.

Definitions

[1] **Ecclesiology** – The study of the identity and function of the church.

WEEK 12: SUMMARY AND CONCLUSION

As we conclude this study, we begin by recapping the big picture of 1 Corinthians as a whole. We will then review some questions for reflection in light of the book's entire message, with a final identification of Gospel Glimpses, Whole-Bible Connections, and Theological Soundings, all with a view to appreciating Paul's first biblical letter to the Corinthians in its entirety.

▶ The Big Picture of 1 Corinthians

During our study of this letter, we detected the main theme of *gospel unity*. The letter began by informing the reader that this church was fractured and needed its vision of the gospel restored and, consequently, its unity rebuilt around Jesus. The letter is quite practical all the way through, but in chapters 1–4 a baseline theological reality involving proclamation, wisdom, and unity is established, while chapters 5–15 apply that vision to practical matters of behavior and belief.

Chapters 1–4 are a powerful rebuke and encouragement, using some of the most elevated language in Scripture with regard to the cross and its implications for Christian character. The Corinthians were divided, with factions following different Christian leaders (1:10–17a). The underlying issue was pride due to a lack of understanding of God's sovereign and infinite grace. This pride fostered self-sufficiency, elitism, competitiveness, and thus disunity. There were cultural and social pressures, and the Corinthians were giving way to those pressures out of a superficial understanding of the gospel. Paul's response was to show them that the gospel turned their worldview upside down, that all that they thought was wise and powerful was actually weak, and that God's wisdom and power were made known through the death of his Son upon the cross, as proclaimed by humble preachers (1:17b–4:21).

Chapters 5–15 take up practical matters, some of which were occasioned by a previous interchange of letters that are not included in the Bible. From sexual purity, to legal cases; from issues of marriage, divorce, and betrothal, to food and idolatry; from worship order to the truth of the bodily resurrection, Paul uses the baseline argument of chapters 1–4 to expose, rebuke, rebuild, and encourage gospel unity and godliness.

Paul concludes his letter with a brief yet powerful reminder about his effort to collect money for the poor in the Jerusalem church, a vivid expression of gospel unity in that a Gentile church was sacrificing to help a Jewish church (16:1–24).

The first section of 1 Corinthians (chs. 1–4) teaches that true power, wisdom, and worth are in Christ crucified. The second section (chs. 5–15) teaches that the cross changes our view of all activities, personal and communal. Paul anchors his letter in the truth of the resurrection, reminding us that the power of the cross was vindicated, fulfilled, and released in the resurrection of Jesus. Throughout the letter, we are reminded that this glorious cross and resurrection truth brings about loving unity among believers (13:1–13). (For further background, see the *ESV Study Bible*, pages 2187–2191, or visit www.esvbible.org.)

Read through the following three sections on *Gospel Glimpses, Whole-Bible Connections*, and *Theological Soundings*. Then take time to reflect on the *Personal Implications* these sections may have for your walk with the Lord.

▶ Gospel Glimpses

In our journey through 1 Corinthians we have been reminded about how the gospel of God's free grace, made known through Jesus, draws believers together as a loving and unified family. Because the Corinthian church had embraced a superficial gospel, their community was fracturing, allowing cultural values to press in on them, divisions to rise around gifted leaders, lawsuits to be used against other believers, and many other divisive issues to arise, including sexual immorality. In the first chapters Paul encapsulates the main idea: the gospel is foolishness to a world that is premised on human power, but it is the actual wisdom and power of God that confounds human wisdom. Once the Corinthians— and we—embrace that reality, not only is our vision of God made right, but also our love for one another is unleashed. Thus, we see in 1 Corinthians a gospel that unites people not around reciprocity or affinity, but around the reality of a crucified Savior, who gave his life as a ransom for many (Matt. 20:28).

Has 1 Corinthians helped shape your understanding of the gospel in a new way? How?

Were there any particular passages or themes in 1 Corinthians that led you to have a fresh understanding and grasp of God's grace to us through Jesus? What about the theme of grace as it relates to Christian unity?

Whole-Bible Connections

First Corinthians is a New Testament letter, and thus a theological and pastoral communication to the early church on how to apply the ministry of Jesus to their lives. Along with the other New Testament letters, it helps answer the question, "What does the kingdom under the Savior King look like?" Paul quotes or alludes to the Old Testament at several points to make his arguments, but the overall theme of unity around the grace of God is a continuation of a central biblical thread. In fact, the way that Paul sets the stage for the entire letter in chapters 1–4 is an extended reflection on common themes of the Old Testament, especially the very notion of a Creator, from whom all things exist and find their being and who is the only one who gets credit in human giftedness and power (1 Cor. 4:7; 8:6). All of the whole-Bible themes in this letter are connected to this "true power" theme, as they are in the rest of the Scriptures.

How has your understanding of the place of 1 Corinthians in the sweep of the Bible been deepened through this study?

Did you see any particular connections to the Old Testament in 1 Corinthians that are new to you?

How has your understanding of the themes of "true power" and "true unity" been enhanced through your study of 1 Corinthians?

How has 1 Corinthians clarified and established the unity of the entire Bible for you?

What development has your study of this letter brought about in your view of who Jesus is and how he fulfills the Old Testament?

▶ Theological Soundings

Several important Christian doctrines are developed and reinforced in 1 Corinthians, such as the bodily resurrection of Christ and Christians, the gifts and administration of the Holy Spirit, the role of preaching, the Lord's Supper, Christian identity, the need for sexual purity, and eschatology.

Has your understanding of Christian theology been developed, or changed, by your study of 1 Corinthians? If so, how?

How have you grown in your understanding of God and his character?

What truths does 1 Corinthians teach in a unique way such that, without this letter, your understanding of the person and work of Jesus would be impoverished?

What, specifically, does 1 Corinthians teach about the human condition and our need for redemption?

Personal Implications

As you consider 1 Corinthians as a whole, what implications do you see for your own life? Consider especially the issue of Christian unity. What are the ramifications—for yourself and for your relationship with others and with God—from Paul's teaching in 1 Corinthians on the reality of the gospel?

What implications for life flow from your reflections on the questions already asked in this week's study concerning Gospel Glimpses, Whole-Bible Connections, and Theological Soundings?

What have you learned in 1 Corinthians that might lead you to praise God, turn away from sin, or trust more firmly in his promises?

As You Finish Studying 1 Corinthians . . .

We rejoice with you as you finish studying the letter of 1 Corinthians! May the wisdom gained through this study become part of your Christian walk of faith, day by day and week by week throughout all your life. Now we would greatly encourage you to study the Word of God on a week-by-week basis. To continue your study of the Bible, we would encourage you to consider other books in the *Knowing the Bible* series, and to visit www.knowingthebibleseries.org.

Lastly, take a moment to look back through this study. Review the notes that you have written, and the things that you have highlighted or underlined. Reflect again on the key themes that the Lord has been teaching you about himself and about his Word. May these things become a treasure for you throughout your life—this we pray in the name of the Father, and the Son, and the Holy Spirit. Amen.